Contents

Why are bugs athletic?

Bugs need to be good at running, jumping, swimming and flying so they can escape from danger and find food or a mate.

Locusts are supreme athletes. They are good high jumpers and long jumpers, and can fly marathon distances.

The click **beetle** is like a pole vaulter. If it falls on to its back, it uses a spring under its body to leap up into the air and turn the right way up.

Some bugs are much better **athletes** than people. The most athletic have long legs, big **muscles** and strong wings to help them move.

A click beetle actually makes a loud CLICK! when it jumps.

Sprint champions

The long legs of these cockroaches help them to scuttle quickly into hiding if they sense danger.

Fast runners usually have long legs so they can take big strides and cover a lot of ground quickly.

If there were running races in a Bug Olympics, the champions would probably be **cockroaches**, **sun spiders** and tiger beetles.

Sun spiders can run in short bursts at speeds of up to 16 km/h in search of bugs to eat. Can you run that fast?

Spider gymnasts

Most spiders are brilliant **gymnasts**. They spin thin lines of **silk**, climbing up and down them like circus performers.

Some spiders have hairy feet that stick to smooth surfaces. They can climb up glass or hang upside down.

One, two, three...go! A jumping spider leaps into the air, using its silk as a safety line in case it falls.

Other spiders use different gymnastic skills to escape from danger.

Here is a golden wheel spider doing a cartwheel down a sand dune.

This is the golden wheel spider with its legs stretched out fully.

9

Wonder walkers

A centipede's long legs lift its long body clear of the ground, which helps it move faster.

The word centipede means 'one hundred legs' but centipedes may have as few as 30 legs or as many as 350 legs.

Centipedes have lots of legs, which help them to sprint fast after **prey** or run away from danger.

A millipede has even more legs than a centipede, but this doesn't make it a faster runner. If a centipede and a millipede were to have a race, the centipede would always win.

A millipede's legs are shorter than a centipede's. It doesn't move them all at the same time. It has to move them in waves or it would trip up!

Long *jumpers*

The huge muscles at the top of this grasshopper's back legs are the power behind its big jumps.

Grasshoppers, locusts and crickets have big back legs for jumping. It's quicker than walking! Jumping also helps them to escape danger.

Powerful muscles straighten out the legs to lift the bug high above the ground.

If you could jump as far as a locust, you would probably be able to jump right across your classroom in a single leap!

To take off, these bugs may leap high into the air, then open their wings and fly away.

13

High jumpers

Fleas have little elastic pads at the base of their legs, which catapult them into the air. When they land, they can bounce back again straight away.

For their size, fleas can jump higher than any other animal.

Springtails have a forked 'tail' under the body that pushes against the ground to throw them up into the air.

Other bugs that are good at the high jump include froghoppers, leafhoppers, springtails and flea beetles.

If you could jump as high as a flea, you would be able to jump over buildings taller than a house!

Bug ballet

On their short, stumpy legs, **butterfly** and **moth caterpillars** are not very speedy. But they sometimes look like graceful dancers.

Looper caterpillars bend their long bodies into loops as they walk along. They have to do this because they have no legs in the middle.

Some caterpillars look like they are dancing together. They follow each other in long lines to search for food or a safe place to change into moths.

Loopers are also called inchworms because they move along inch by inch – often quite fast.

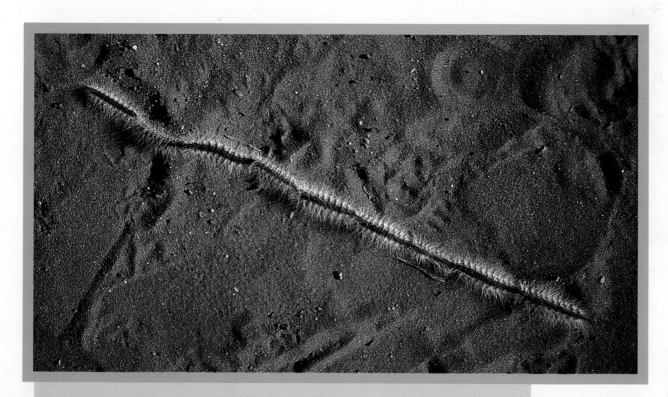

These pine processionary moth caterpillars look as if they are dancing in a long conga line.

17

Strong-bug contestants

This pair of dung beetles are pushing a huge ball of animal dung. They use it as food for their young grubs.

Some bugs need to be very strong to win a mate and provide food for their young.

Male beetles sometimes fight each other over females. The strongest beetle wins the wrestling match and the mate.

A rhinoceros beetle can support 850 times its own weight on its back. A human weightlifter can lift three times his own weight above his head.

Male stag beetles wrestle with their massive jaws. Each beetle tries to lift his rival into the air and smash him to the ground.

Weightlifters

Beetles are not the only bugs with superhuman strength. Other bugs also lift heavy weights.

This bee-killer wasp is carrying food home for her young – a very heavy honeybee.

This ant is carrying a **pupa** to a safe place. Inside the pupa, an ant grub is changing into an adult.

Leafcutter ants carry big pieces of leaf back to their nest to turn into food. They can carry pieces many times their own size.

Even though **ants** look thin and weedy, they are strong for their size. They often work together to carry heavy loads.

Leafcutter ants often carry tiny ants on their leaves too. These are the minors, there to protect their big sisters from attack.

Air acrobats

Flies such as this bluebottle can land upside down and walk upside down across the ceiling.

A hoverfly can hover on the spot. It has two little joysticks instead of back wings to help it balance and steer. Can you see one in this picture?

The best fliers in the bug world are **flies** and dragonflies. They twist and turn through the air like tiny helicopters.

Dragonflies are more agile than any bird or aeroplane. They have two pairs of wings, which beat up and down about 20 times a second.

How many times can you blink in a second? In the same time, some flies can beat their wings a thousand times!

A dragonfly can fly backwards and forwards, **hover**, turn round sharply and come to an instant stop.

Flight specialists

Hawk moths are like tiny jet planes. Air flows easily over the narrow, pointed wings of a hawk moth, helping it to fly fast.

Some hawk moths reach speeds of up to 50 km/h. That's as fast as a car!

A hawk moth beats its wings so fast that its wings are usually a blur. A camera can barely capture them in a photograph.

The hummingbird hawk moth eats and flies at the same time. It hovers on one spot while sipping flower nectar with its long tongue.

The two wings on each side are clipped together by very small, bristly hairs. This helps the moth save energy when flying.

Marathon monarchs

Monarchs glide on the wind to save energy. They also float upwards on rising currents of warm air, just like hang-gliders.

The champion of the bug **marathon** has to be the monarch butterfly. It flies 3,000 km in one journey, travelling up to 200 km in a day.

In Mexico, the green trees are turned orange and brown because there are millions of butterflies clinging to the branches.

On their return journey, the butterflies lay their eggs and die. Their offspring finish the journey back to Canada.

To escape the cold winters in Canada, huge numbers of monarch butterflies fly south to Mexico. In the spring, they fly north towards Canada again.

Super swimmers

Great diving beetles are strong swimmers. They row themselves through the water using their two wide, flat back legs.

Hairy fringes on the legs brush a lot of water aside as they sweep the beetle along.

The adult beetles have **streamlined** bodies, which cut through the water easily and help them to swim fast.

Great diving beetles are all-round athletes. They are good at flying as well as swimming.

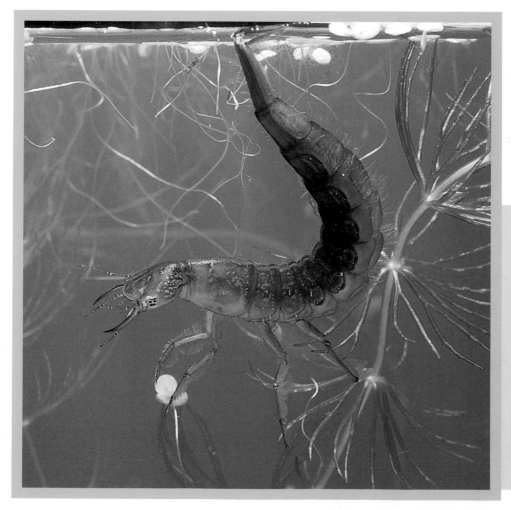

The young, or larva, of the great diving beetle also has hairy legs, which work like oars to help it swim.

29

Words to remember

ant A small insect that lives with other ants in a large group called a colony.

athlete Someone who is good at sports and exercises.

beetle A flying insect with tough front wings that cover most of its body like a case.

bug The word 'bug' can be used to mean any type of minibeast. A true bug is a type of insect with a stabbing beak.

butterfly A flying insect that usually flies by day and has brightly coloured wings.

caterpillar A young butterfly or moth.

centipede A long minibeast (not an insect) with many legs and poisonous claws.

cockroach A tough, flat insect, with long legs. Most can fly.

dragonfly A large flying insect that eats other insects and rests with its wings spread out.

flea A tiny jumping insect that cannot fly. Fleas feed on animal blood.

fly A flying insect with only two wings.

grasshopper A jumping insect with long, powerful back legs. It usually has wings too.

gymnast Someone good at exercises in the gym.

hover To hang in the air over one spot.

insect A minibeast with three parts to its body and six legs. Most insects can fly.

locust A large grasshopper, which jumps and flies well.

marathon A long distance race needing great strength and staying power.

moth A flying insect that usually flies at night and is usually a dull colour.

muscles The parts of an animal's body that produce movement.

prey An animal that is killed or eaten by another animal.

pupa A resting stage in the life cycle of some insects, during which they change shape and grow wings.

silk A fibre made by spiders and some insects to make safety lines, webs or cocoons.

spider A minibeast (not an insect) with eight legs and two poisonous fangs.

streamlined A smooth, slim shape, which cuts through air or water easily.

sun spider A speedy minibeast related to spiders (but not a spider). It usually lives in dry places and hunts insects at night.

Index